Nan and Pop

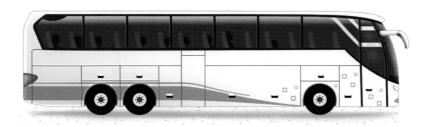

Nan and Pop get off the bus. We hug Nan and Pop.

Pop has a red box and Nan has a big bag.

6

Is the box for us, Pop?
Yes, it is muffins for us.

Is the bag for us, Nan?
No, it is for Pam.

Pam is in luck.
She licks the bag.

Pam digs at the bag.
She is quick. She rips it.

Yum! Yum!
It is a win for Pam
and a win for us.

Before reading

Say the sounds: c k ck j qu v w x y z zz ff ll ss
Ensure the children use the pure sounds for the consonants without the added "uh" sound, e.g. "llll" not "luh".

Practise blending the sounds: Nan bag luck win rips quick muffins Pop bus licks us red box hug digs yes yum Pam

High-frequency words: at big off and in it get

Tricky words: we no she for is has the

Vocabulary check: luck – What does "good luck" or "bad luck" mean? Can children give some examples?

Story discussion: Look at the cover illustration and read the title. Discuss who this story is about. What are other names children know that can be used for grandparents? (e.g. gran, grandpa, nonna, etc.)

Teaching points: Review the tricky words "is", "his", "as" and "has". Explain that the tricky part is the "s" which has a /z/ sound in these words. When "s" follows a vowel or a voiced consonant it will have the /z/ sound. Look at other examples such as logs, lads, tubs, buns, rags, kids. Also look at examples where the "s" follows a voiceless consonant and so has the /s/ sound, e.g. rips, taps, hits, gets, licks. Review double letters/two-syllable words (muffins). Review /kw/ sound for qu (quick).

After reading

Comprehension:
- What did Pop have in his box?
- What did Nan have in her bag?
- What did Pam do to the bag?
- How was it a "win" for the kids and Pam?

Fluency: Speed read the words again from the inside front cover.